"This book is a rare treasure! The poems radiate powerful light that comes from the author's great heart, authentic wisdom, and beautiful way with words. Rich with courage, honesty, and grace, these poems will surely light your life."

—T. A. Barron, author of The Merlin Saga

"S.A. Borders-Shoemaker's poems and meditations in *Waiting for Scotland* are whispers of wisdom and insight gathered like leaves on a tree to give wandering souls a blessing of shade in the fury and heat of our day. *Waiting for Scotland* has three branches—'Packing Bags,' 'Bravehearted Plans,' and 'Different Hopes'—that give different perspectives to a wanderer's journey. Each branch filled with wisdom and insight, *Waiting for Scotland* is a journey waiting to be taken."

—W. Michael Farmer, PhD

"These beautifully written, intimate poems, spoken from a heart scored with sorrow, breathe with urgency. S.A. Borders-Shoemaker writes of the fragility of life, of being at war with herself for caring about someone who cares little for her.
"Written with this author's characteristic wisdom and hopefulness, Borders-Shoemaker writes, too, of finding good, a true love, and the freedom to be herself with a fearless voice known only to her generation.
"Readers will journey with her as she strives to exist in sadness, trying to survive the moment while feeling nothing. S.A. Borders-Shoemaker tells us 'Our wounds do not define us.' *Waiting for Scotland* holds true to that promise and gives us so very much more."

—Ann Falcone Shalaski, author of *World Made of Glass*, *Without Pretense*, and *Just So You Know*

<u>More praise for *Waiting for Scotland*</u>

"Her poems are gritty, earthy and yet belong to the stars that hold our dreams. In *Waiting for Scotland*, S.A. Borders-Shoemaker's honesty and insight are breathtaking. Great poets meet you at the crossroads of your deepest thoughts, at the places where you feel the pluck of each nerve, where hope and uncertainty trade. S.A. Borders-Shoemaker will speak to places you didn't know you had, evoke emotion you didn't believe possible. She doesn't just write poetry—as far as I can tell, she is poetry."

—Jeffrey Blount, author of *The Emancipation of the Walls*

"S.A. Borders-Shoemaker calls her *Waiting for Scotland* 'Poems and Meditations.' Written with intensity, these compact works comprise a woman's rite of passage from a history of fear and abuse—the poet doesn't tell us what kind of abuse, but there are hints that it was both physical and verbal—to a fully realized adult capable of freeing herself from the traumas of her past and finding inner strength to risk vulnerability, thereby opening herself to accepting and giving love. But first she must confront and speak her truth, which she finds painful and terrifying. 'Pain is a place / where truth / has trouble speaking. / And I / have often been silent.'

"Part I, which the poet calls 'Packing Bags,' is turned upside down into the narrator's unpacking her psychological bags. Scotland functions not only as the geographical place that the narrator is waiting to visit, but also as a metaphor for her therapeutic journey into herself. And she is not going to wait for this inner trip to happen. The entire collection of writings in this volume depicts a proactive narrator working her way through her past and present, laying preparation for a more hopeful future. There are many memorable, sometimes powerful lines as the narrator struggles to speak her truth.

"In Part II, 'Bravehearted Plans,' the poet proclaims, 'Everything is a poem / if you allow it / to speak.' Borders-Shoemaker angrily decries the humiliating dilemma so many women experience in a patriarchal culture where women are defined—and thereby subjugated—by men. 'Don't wait for / someone / to proclaim your worth / It's already yours.' Titles of some of the short poems function as road signs along this biographical journey: 'control and love aren't the same thing;' 'it takes guts to be who you are;' 'there is no love without liberty.'

"In Part III, 'Different Hopes,' the poem's narrator achieves her longing for fulfillment at all the complex multilevel aspects of her human nature—intellectual, sexual, emotional, creative. The metaphor of the journey to Scotland is fully immersed in the narrator's journey into herself."

—Mary Batten, author of *Life in Hot Water:*
Wildlife at the Bottom of the Ocean

S.A. BORDERS-SHOEMAKER

WAITING
—— FOR ——
SCOTLAND
POEMS AND MEDITATIONS

BELLE ISLE BOOKS
www.belleislebooks.com

Copyright © 2022 by S.A. Borders-Shoemaker

No part of this book may be reproduced in any form or by any electronic or mechanical means, or the facilitation thereof, including information storage and retrieval systems, without permission in writing from the publisher, except in the case of brief quotations published in articles and reviews. Any educational institution wishing to photocopy part or all of the work for classroom use, or individual researchers who would like to obtain permission to reprint the work for educational purposes, should contact the publisher.

ISBN: 978-1-958754-02-3
LCCN: 2022914085

Photography by Tianna Yentzer

Printed in the United States of America

Published by
Belle Isle Books (an imprint of Brandylane Publishers, Inc.)
5 S. 1st Street
Richmond, Virginia 23219

BELLE ISLE BOOKS
www.belleislebooks.com

belleislebooks.com | brandylanepublishers.com

To my beloved, Tim,
&
In loving memory of Doris Rea Gwaltney

TABLE OF CONTENTS

BRAVEHEARTED PLANS

She asked me—
What if you wrote without apology,
without shame?
Remove the filters—
what would you say?
So, I did,
and this is what I said.
                              —therapist/method

I
PACKING BAGS

It was our deal—
tickets in pockets
and a trip to Scotland,
time and toasts
to the life ahead.

Along the way,
notes waft from
other nooks in my soul,
memories of before
and those closer to now.

In preparing to leave,
the words fill me,
like incense and burning sage,
a hunger and a pit
in my stomach to ease.

What can I do
when lost letters
return themselves
and demand answers
amid my wanderings?
Only this:
consider their proposal
and start somewhere
in the before and
after.
—*a story old and new*

I tell myself,
write it down,
but I am so very,
dreadfully—
afraid.
—*but, oh, how I want to say the truth*

How can it be
that without any
physical evidence
my jaw feels broken,
my rib cage crushed?
Maybe it lies
in the hedges of words
and pressure
from people
who were supposed to
love me.
—*blood doesn't make loyalty*

Don't rush it,
an inward voice tells me.
The words will be ready when it's time
to tell your story.
Don't be overeager
to pour your soul's wine.
It must first ferment,
then lie down to rest
and be encased in wisdom.
—the wine of confession

Mercy,
be kind in this moment
and come to my aid,
before I make a wreckage
of myself again.
I have no need for the needle gun.
My heart is already tattooed
with your words
and the ones I write on it.
—*mercy's mark*

My mind's eye sees
betwixt the sockets
of some man's skull—
there, on the family mantle,
my great grandfather's glasses
rest on its bridgeless nose.
Funny
that I know the image
but neither man.
—*the familiar unknown*

It's a DNA duality of
caring and insecurity,
the drive to succeed,
stunted by dry soul wells,
long unattended
and poisoned with decay.

This ball of emotions
inside my chest—
wet with the weight of
compassion, fatigue,
and fear—
is your legacy in me.

Hesitation—
hiding, simmering rage,
waiting,
the ambition
pulling
my judgment apart.

You are maker and
breaker of me,
a pillar and fissure,
a foundation I embrace
with fear and love.

Every dawn is a
moment to decide
which I invite in—
the good you left
or the illness we created.
—*inherited*

The tap of fingers
undecided on their course
ring out in the living room.
Is it time
to tell the story,
or is my vision
still too fixated
on one side?
—*pertinent questions*

Fear
often covers
my mouth
because I don't want to harm.
—*I've seen what words can do*

This thing to adorn,
a stone on third finger—
for Cicero, perhaps
even myself,
speaks, calls, extends from
a past and future,
bound in soul blood.
—*own your life's story*

Before you come,
understand that I am afraid,
that the shattered glass on the floors
of the temple in which you will walk
is being made into mosaics.

Before you open the door,
know your presence
is a disturbance,
that these halls are hallowed
with restful silence.

Before you step inside,
note the guard dog
that beckons your entrance
but smacks his lips,
awaiting your misstep.

Before you come in,
remember that this home isn't yours.
Our shared blood
does not make you master of this house.
I am its keeper.
—*before you come home*

I know the road
better than any home.
With isolation as my mantle,
I can't escape the cold.
And I struggle
with the thought
of a land called
mother.
—*a map with no end*

I can expect you
every half hour
through day and night
to berate me—
Unworthy, dumb bitch,
godless pretender:
come back to your abusers,
it's all you deserve.
—texts from the known

Pain is a place
where truth
has trouble speaking.
And I
have often been silent.
—*closed-mouth lessons*

Grief looked like anger
for a long while,
and I smashed mirrors
of social interaction
seeking the truth.
—*pain in action*

Picture it—
a forest of words
grows in my mouth,
rooted and gnarled and
dark, brilliant patches of light
cutting through canopied reservations.

It is easier
to be a handmaiden of sorrow
than to question and hope
for a circumstance beyond
this veiled present.

The leaves in my speech,
scrawled with words and secrets,
cover those hidden pathways—
a forest floor of lost meaning.

Would I wish not
for easier sojourns and
open skies?
(Save that I become steadfast
in the realms of uncertainty.)
If my words are dense,
consider the trees—
their shade and gifts of air—
and better know
what I can offer,
an oddity of salves.
—*hard to say*

When I gaze
at the pages of history,
I ask future pens
to be kind,
though it's a futile request.
—*the harshness of historians*

There were dreams
waking among the green
hills and roadsides,
of falling in love and becoming
someone different—
another version of myself without
the past.
I am changed now—
a form of me with a different story,
and the only love left empty
is for a country I cannot have.
—*forever the foreigner*

There I am—
in faded colors on a bench,
yet my laugh is just as vibrant
as the green soda bottle in my hand.

There it is—
that wild, golden hair—
matched with a love knot necklace.
If only those promises of green were eternal.

There they are—
the remnants of filial safety
that even now I do not possess—
not even in mental photographs.
—*a bench and a photo in St. Andrews*

Forever my words
are woven with magic,
and to tragedy
I bring beautiful words
and give life meaning.
Does loveliness make it any less true?
—*beauty doesn't mean deception*

I have said some
stupid things
in my life.

I have done some
foolish acts
over the years.

I have caused some
pain and loss,
even when I didn't mean to.

And that seems to be all you remember.
—*I'm more than my mistakes*

It is not
a polite story,
but then again,
what truth ever was?
—*I don't write for comfort's sake*

Boys, sex,
makeup, and clothing—
privileged topics
for safe families.
—*teenage questions unspoken*

My memory is like a puzzle
with pieces I can't find
until I'm brushed
with sight or feeling;
then the jagged outlines
appear in my palm,
and I search for its place.
—*memory trauma*

Whenever salty air
fills my nostrils,
I am returned to winter
in Sydney's harbor,
near the churning of dark water.

I wander Lyme Regis;
my hair is a banner,
a tribute to hurting hearts,
iced waves smacking against
man-made walls by the ocean.

I stand on East Beach,
beside the fogged waters of Georgia,
running with full force
to hide in that density,
fleeing where I didn't belong.

I walk by the river
that colonialism made famous
and only have to wonder
what kind of storm
is rolling off the James.
—*smell has a memory*

Hands press,
slam,
against the walls of mortality—
a room that can swell and
contract
with the wellness of my mind.
—*understanding brevity*

Funny,
breath is not measured
until panic is near
or its scarcity is learned.
—*missing*

It's the truest confession
to fall from
my sputtering mouth—
I want to be loved.
I want to be good.

His embrace says gently
what his words whisper to
my shaking body,
You already are,
and you are more than enough.
—panic attack

I can feel it,
standing here while you debate
whether you approve,
or do I imagine that?
—*outside approval is a fickle thing*

I shake
beneath the weight of fear,
wondering each and every time
you leave,
Will you abandon me
like they did?
—when loss has been my compass

Does it entertain you—
smashing the petals
of trust that I gave?
You can call me naïve,
but I know the actual word for you.
—*cruel*

It is not
my responsibility
to shoulder your consequences.
For all your age,
this is a childish expectation.
—*Sin Eater*

There is a room
filled with old and new things,
but when I go to grab what is mine,
you're standing there—
my accuser with a bloodied whip
claiming all I see.
—*fighting for the narrative*

Revelation strikes
like glorious lightning
or a simple question:
But really, what do you think?
—I want to know, too

Pause.
Not every
moment
deserves a reaction.
—*resist the instigator*

The line of
family history
is the scrawl of
terrified people
searching to end
the hurt.

It is sealed
with waxed silence
and eyes askance
from the monster,
keeping us cornered.

Until the moment
when it couldn't have
me.
—*breaking the curse*

I don't understand
what my dress
has to do with you—
I wear it for myself.

I don't understand
what my makeup
has to do with my ideas—
my mind is sharp.

I don't understand
what you think
empowers you to control my appearance—
I can be both beautiful and intelligent.
—*female academics can't be pretty*

If the story
is written by
my own hand,
then I
must learn the
value of a pause.
—*there is wisdom in rest*

And what am I protecting—
years of heartache,
a wound with whispered names,
a torn portrait on a heartflesh wall?
No.
It's the dream
I still wish
to never have
buried.
—*mute*

A lie meant to hurt him
and wound me
brought men with guns
and a false sense of justice
to our home.
It takes everything
to tell
bare-breasted truth
calmly,
even when it is correct.
—*lies and guns don't correct abuse*

How fitting it is
that our empire fell
like a castle torched
or a surgery botched,
but still stands in pieces.

We are the charred branches
of powerful but ruined roots,
remnants of former greatness,
heralds of self-destruction
too proud to transform.

And what did we lose in this war—
our history or belonging,
communication and lineage,
even identity?

How appropriate it is—
a shell of an ancestral home
echoing my former name,
that mad physician cutting up myself.

In the halls of Dunalastair, I paid
for my fealty, my love,
and I burned—
our ghosts confined by
dead walls.

And still, I wonder amid
these grave-silent ashes:
How can this destruction
surprise you
when hands of blood hold the flame?
—Dunalastair

Fingers reach,
cold and dirty,
for a comfort
no longer there—
but a kind of love is;
it always will be.
—*regardless*

II
BRAVEHEARTED
PLANS

With ticket in hand,
I await
the moment to
leave
and arrive.

What I've wanted
and doggedly pursued
seems to morph
and move away
from my hands.

Where I think I belong
isn't the case—
yet here I am,
bags beside me still.
—*waiting for Scotland*

Raindrops speckle a
quilted blanket on grass,
ivory pages of a leather notebook,
and cups full
of something stronger than
steeped leaves and sugar.

Take my hand
and a seat beside.
I'll tell you dark and
wonderful tales—
secrets and dreamscapes
from places far and cherished.

Feel the pull
of love and
spiritual warmth,
hands full of careful words
crafted for adventure and connection.

Holders without candles,
brass rounds reflecting
clouded sun and misty light,
illumine our future
with unseen flame.

Have my promise
laced around your heart,
a beautiful shield
made of tougher things
and softer truths.

This, our life,

a picnic in the rain—
resilient in grief,
a strange and
beautiful thing.
—*beauty in hardship*

I cannot undo
damage from the
knives they drew—
only stich myself
together again,
an entity anew.
—*creating me again*

I am a
woman of silence.
Words are
the harvest of
my thoughts.
—*may your harvest bring life*

I want to understand,
redeem, even
these harsh words—
but time and again,
their purpose is clear:
only for harm, for control.
—*control and love aren't the same thing*

My words
are not witch hunts,
just burdens
to be set free.
—*judge not*

Feel the fear,
but remember:
it is not
your master.
—*I control my reaction*

Run, beloved.
The hounds of your dreamscape
howl for the chase but
will not catch you!

The jailers jeer and yell, yet
your laughter drowns
them, mirth triumphant—
how sweet is your morningtide escape!

A dress of blue and white
falls to your heels,
a celebration of
love and beauty in this moment.

Chase the sunbeams
beyond the trees—
they are the future
that you've won in choosing.

Do not fear, love!
Your feet and soulwork
will bear away
this body to a new homeland.
—*dreamscapes*

I speak these truths
for the knowledge,
the boldness,
that you can—

Speak
so that walls
will fall
and liberate.
—*the commission*

Have the courage
to be
that unique part
of yourself
others don't
have to understand.
—*it takes guts to be who you are*

Here I am,
casually as ever,
whispering lyrics from
the Police,
sipping on my coffee—
slightly sweet, ever consistent.
—*Cure, the coffee haunt*

On this side of the world,
the one where I was born,
I still feel disconnected.
With all my wandering,
my tribe is scattered,
and sometimes I just want
to see their faces without a screen.
—*worlds apart*

With bloodied lip,
get up and fight again,
if for no one else
than yourself,
to save, to redeem the sear
of your affliction.
—*woman, the warrior*

There are whispers,
ashen with fear,
of a world dying.
I don
a billed mask and say,
Not yet.
—we've survived before

The crowned sickness
points its illusive dagger
in my direction,
so I dress in armor
and wait in my wooden castle,
surrounded by a sacrifice-filled moat.
—*outwaiting the siege*

Everything is a poem
if only you allow it
to speak.
So listen carefully.
—*poetry is*

You think I write
of former lovers
and spurned hopes.
How dull and
unimaginative—
a single lens
for a
kaleidoscope experience.
—*not what you think*

Sitting in the grass,
I stare off into
the misty haze above the river
that wafts through the trees,
realizing my world
is both silent and moving.
With numbed body and
unmoving lips,
I am still
waiting for answers.
—*fatigue*

I still regret
all that I lost
to pledge my fealty
to the blood members
under the pretense
of true loyalty.
—*accepting my consequences*

Do not mistake me.
It took time and
great work, pain,
to speak as I do now.

My words have been
whetted and pointed,
but they have not only
cut,
they have
also sewn back together.

Regardless of your opinions—
I do not mean to be unkind—
I long to say
what only the walls of my mouth
have contained.
—*this is not about you*

In contemplation,
I see my many
mistakes.
In forgiveness,
I see the possibility
of who I could be.
—*reworking the reflection*

Change is
a time for
bravado.
So I did
what I couldn't before:
I left the abuse and lies.
—*survivor/heroine*

I did not want
to write this letter.
We were thrown into
a chaotic, sticky mess.

I gave my youth to you.

You allowed
a teenage girl
to take on
the burden.

A physical ocean separates us,
not just
the spiritual chasm
that already existed.

I was tired.

I was exhausted.
I wanted you
to be my—
You wanted me gone.

Without shame.

You chose
to disown me.
You sit there and
laugh at this letter.

Laugh at
my vulnerability,

enjoying that
you've hurt me.

I never intended to hurt you.

Please
forgive me,
for when I did,
I hurt, too.

I have allowed
my tears.
I have allowed
my pain.

I forgive you.

I forgive you
anyway.
I forgive you
for me.

I give you
prayers but also
distance.
Go in peace.
—*recipients known, names undisclosed*

You tried to
break my will.
I broke
your chains.
Which of us is the victim now?
—*I won't be enslaved to the wound*

With hearts rendered
open,
let's see each other plainly.
Our distance can finally
be
honest and unburdened.
If only you're willing to admit it.
—*forgiveness and reconciliation are separate*

Strange
to release a birth cord
and find myself secure—
a wild and unexpected
possibility
that sets us both free.
—*what forgiveness looks like*

Love does not get
to be forever untouched.
Sometimes, it is a fight
to be kept alive,
a cooling ember
that lives beneath ashes,
an unspoken knowing.
—*rethinking the matter*

Love was there
and might be still,
with a permanently altered face.
I have the right to choose
this time.
—*there is no love without liberty*

I can forgive you—
do forgive you.
Keeping space
helps us both.
This is a cycle
that won't stop unless we do.
—*boundaries*

I am not the
cold woman
perceived.
Just someone
who looked abuse
in the eye
and said: *no more.*
—*I am my own protection*

Looking at my womb,
I wonder if I am broken.
Can I overcome
the shattered line
before me?
Then she takes my hand
with a knowing glance
and says,
You are not who they are.
—we create our fate

Run through with flame,
the brand of separation,
and my heart was burned.

Fragrance diffused
my wound, fashioning
a small, ornamental lily.

I carried it with me,
through mountain, through sea,
and it was my memory of strength unknown.

The flower became a charm,
blessing assailants,
holding filial love.

For in its beauty, there was a silence—
an alliance unspoken
that bound us together.

My injury was strength
because it showed me
that my own human nature
bound me to my enemy.
—*the lily*

The lens you choose
to look through
becomes your oracle.
Make your predictions hopeful.
—*a word of cautious encouragement*

Don't wait for
someone
to proclaim your worth.
It's already yours.
—*You are worthy. Full stop.*

So often
women are told to be quiet
under other masks.

You're being a bitch.

Because I know
that pain,
I do not begrudge other women.

She took your success.

When assessing a new face,
I will give women
the luxury men have.
—*I will judge them for their ideas*

I realized that
perfection was
the poison
killing my unique soul.
So I spat it out
and lit the rest aflame.
—*unite and conquer*

Friend,
your broken pieces
are the chain mail
for new armor.
Claim
Your
Freedom.
—*don't let them rob you of peace*

The body has
amazing memory.
Even when I lack confidence,
fearing the time lapsed,
it goes to work
remembering what it's made for.
—*the body is a divine creation*

When I am broken,
I look at the phoenix feathers
of my hair
and know I can be reborn—
it's been done before.

When my soul feels crushed,
I paint my mouth
crimson,
knowing my words are flames
that can warm or burn.

When battle is before me,
I wear and
shod myself
in that shade of spice
to remember my victories, present and past.

Why do you think red is my beloved color?
—*the red woman survives*

I found
you
when I let
vulnerability
in.
The most terrifying and joyous reward.
—*take the right leap*

It is a strange moment
when I speak
and am heard.
Such a novelty
to not be punished for
my words.
—*trust over history*

Broken
for the light within
to burst forth.
I am the ground
that nourishes
budding flowers
of witness.
—*potential*

You crack open
the geode of my heart
without word or song
to reveal vulnerable brilliance.
It's a simple invitation—
you standing there
with outstretched arms,
wanting me in spite of myself.
—*when I forget to be soft*

Till the soil,
sow by hand
alongside steady arms
and seasoned life.
I believe in
the sweat of our bodies
that wets the dirt
with joint effort.
—*our garden*

I can't see peppermints
without thinking they should be
in my pocket,
a ready offering.
After all this time,
I'm still prepared
to spoil
those large beasts.
—*the age of horses*

I held you close,
my rust-colored star;
never did I dream
we would part
or you'd grow old.

My first knowledge
that life ends
but love is eternal,
that giving
comes back,
and that I could be brave.
—*R.S.*

Here they come—
hooves upon thunder,
the ground swelling
with their sound,
yet I never saw their aim.

What I love
I learned to mourn, to fear
these things I bound myself
up in, to
the very machine of pain.

Alienation
is a sharp sound
in the imagination,
a line that cuts through image,
becoming the focal point
over the original.

Like the charge of cavalry
in a war I didn't know
but knew every battle plan,
this frontline promised destruction
by what I thought I knew.
—*wars behind shut mouths*

III

DIFFERENT HOPES

I am done
with the waiting and delays,
hoping, only then to be smashed
looking to a day
that does not come.

If I spend my life
always waiting for Scotland,
my dreams, like powder,
will dissolve and drown
in the river of stories.

No, this is the moment
to seize and conquer,
to make something new.
My heart, the tapestry
of old longings and new ideas.

Sometimes,
the shores longed-for
are closed behind borders
of broken love,
while others ask
for more time and healing.

Let this be
the prayer and wish,
from my mouth to the sky,
that I may not be broken
by the disappointing realities
and shadow-ridden memories.
—*another course is set*

In the desperate search,
my identity became a ghost,
effervescent and intangible.
When I stopped,
so did the blurred movement,
and there I was—
real and unclothed—
I knew it.
—*mind haze*

Without traveling, I
arrive,
feeling the journey and
respite.
Dear, look where I was
before—
there is a letter waiting for
you.
—*then and now*

Smoke dusts the field,
a wind following
cannon fires,
but I lay my musket
aside and
leave without
white flags,
only a letter
sealed with honesty.
—*over*

Come,
feel the visceral outlines
of a waking dream
that pulse like shivers
and flow like grass
beneath the wind.

Can you hear it—
the baying of
a black dog,
the soft blow of
a horse's nostrils
thrilled for adventure,
trusting the rider's lead?

We make a run for it—
for hope and hard work—
the artist's pen now
in the form of
running beauty,
inescapable and breathtaking.

In this moment, we
can create the future,
where rustic and extravagant
find an unlikely home
in open-sleeved heart
beating, with waltzing rhythm
performed by bare feet.

I must believe
in the vision of
this moment,

that I am not forever
separated from myself
or imagination.

So, come,
inner child now grown.
See yourself as a woman
and reacquaint with
what you truly love.
—*look backward and forward*

Shame
used to be
the story I accepted.
Then I realized
I was wearing
your clothes.
—*taking on what isn't mine*

I am buttons and lace,
feathers, leaves,
and delicate features
mixed with soft colors.

I am the gentlest moments
of spring and fall,
not an extreme
but a movement of wind and song.

I am intricacies
woven into the stars,
looped moons, and minute designs
for close and careful examination.

I am flowers and oak trees
bent in reverence
to the rain—
these are my truest nature.
—*who I am underneath*

Partaking in
the wine I pressed,
my world looks
familiar,
telling me
home has returned.
—*I can be myself*

Words are wildflowers
in the fields of my mind,
and each one spoken
is a bouquet
I have gathered by hand
with care and attention.
Do not reject
what is offered
in love, in good faith.
—*my words are gifts*

Be kind—
the simplest
and best
choice,
regardless.
—*earned, or not*

I only answer
to worthy
names.
All else is
clutter under my feet.
You do not own who I am.
—*don't answer to a name that isn't yours*

I am
flower petal
and flame,
both soft
and powerful.
Your box of expectations is irrelevant.
—*self-acceptance is a discipline*

Yes, I love elegance
just as much as I
adore raw thoughts.
You can cherish
what is suave
and bold.
—*not everything is a dichotomy*

Because I am female,
child underdog was my title,
not frontrunner eligible,
my sweetness barring projected success.
What a foolish thought.
I proved them wrong.
—*PhD, author, poet, community leader*

See your sisters—
the women you
know and don't—
celebrate.
Because the
things we do
together
create
the tapestry of our world.
—*may we never forget each other*

I am the
shake that ass in the kitchen
sort of woman.
The kind of lady
keeping it classy
with a dagger in my garter.
The diplomat
with lips of flame
and a gentle smile.
The lionheart
with body wrapped in pink silk
and broadsword in hand.
—*imagine that, a strong and tender woman*

This world of
soft blankets,
sweet kisses,
and hopeful laughter
is hard to believe.
But it is real.
—*good at the end of the storm*

I say, *Do not give me anything less than love*
that moves your soul.

I did not come here
for rescue or entrapment.
My presence is a choice
I constantly choose,
choose, choose.

I say, *I want nothing less than a heart*
that respects mine.

Any love before
bears no weight here.
Our kingdom serves no other
kings, queens, or lost ones—
just us.

I say, *Come as no less than*
the man you are.
—the condition of romance

We are wildflowers
without season,
love
without time.

You were my
unexpected turn,
the latent wisdom
in a divine revelation.

Our love
is the kind
I never saw coming—
you love every moment of my lifetime.
—*love is patient, love is wise*

Love is
the quiet river
of the soul
that sustains.
Thank God for
its unhurried, forgiving
flow.
—*loved in spite of ourselves*

There's a poem on the wall
where you made vows
and I accepted rings,
sealing what were already
blooming flowers.

Beside it is a map of stars
that cover our month,
meant to navigate oceans
and family wars,
a testimony to commitment.

And close by is a record player
that has seen us dance slowly,
drink joyfully to good,
sing despite circumstance,
and love when it wasn't expected.

This is the home we're creating.
—*I choose to love you*

You are
so rooted
and I, a skyborn being,
play off strengths and
draw up weaknesses
to fashion stable ground
for the future.
—*two sides of the same process*

I turn
diamond-laced rings,
and scattered colors
dapple around my hand.
It is a beauty
I indulge in,
hard fought for the win.
—*we survived, we thrive*

You
made me know
love didn't have to hurt,
that it could be real
and not leave me feeling
bruised.

You
respected,
did not detest them—
the broken pieces of me—
but learned with trembling
to have gentle hands.
—*thank you*

The smell of
oil and batter-wrapped fish
adorned with newspaper and
potato wedges
always transports me
to those stony streets and
misty shores.
—*firsts for Scotland*

In those old streets then,
to this very moment,
the thoughts in Edinburgh
remain true:
my destiny is bound up in words.
—*The Edinburgh Writers' Museum*

In the simplicity of
this life,
I forget that I've sat
among princes and queens
in another time.
Then again,
what does it truly matter
when I am richer now
with love and compassion?
—*know where wealth lies*

You will be heard far and wide,
the handwritten note says
that lays at the bottom of
some forgotten box,
yet the words are ever-present
in these ears and mind.
—*handwritten letters from T. A. B.*

My younger self
knew two things:
*I am a writer
and that is meant to be.*
—some things remain true

Endless
is the love
shown to me
by friends,
by mentors,
and by those who choose.
This is my constant
pride and humility.
—*accept what is given freely*

They say fear
is a monster
wailing and crying out
to tell you the truth.
And my own beast
sits beside me.
I benefit from listening
as it bequeaths
jeweled knowledge.
—*treasures from doing the work*

Here is my apology
to those I have wronged,
for when I have fallen short
and forgotten.
Forgiveness is something you
can take or reject;
regardless, I will take my portion
and dedicate it to becoming
a better self.
—*peace from without and within*

I love the feeling
of soft-bristle brushes
against my hair,
and that is his legacy:
helping me to relax
and remember moments
when I didn't fear touch.
—*how I choose to remember my grandfather*

Don't forget,
she says,
there is fire in your
hair and blood.
This is the heritage
and burden
I accept.
—*bloodlines*

We can't all
just be one thing.
No one is only good,
or forever evil,
or perfectly balanced.
—*acceptance/humanity*

There is a
mark
where the muzzle
used to be.
Sometimes, I
enjoy freedom,
other moments
I forget
that the muzzle is gone.
—*hard to forget*

What I wanted
and what you
were willing to give
are two different things.
I forgive us for it.
—*relationships we want and what we get*

My youth wasn't spent
on dreams of kisses and princes
but rather becoming a hero
for myself and others—
something you would see.
—*imagined possibilities*

I am grateful
to those teachers
of silence and tolerance—
and, sometimes,
they have been foolish me.
—*what Gibran knew*

There have been
many people
I was supposed to be,
many people
I've tried to be.
And the only one
who's worked out
is me.
—*accepting scars and mantles*

There is a place
where rest can be found,
cool and quiet as the river
of peace and solitude,
where one day, maybe
wandering souls will
see their paths
in the water's reflection.

—a writer's benison

ABOUT THE AUTHOR

S.A. Borders-Shoemaker is an author, poet, and PhD in the Hampton Roads region of Virginia. Some influences on her writing include her work in conflict resolution and suicide prevention, as well as her extensive travels abroad. She has over fifteen publications in both national and international outlets, including *Frankenstein & the Phoenix*, *Rooted in Time*, *The Conscious Objection*, and numerous op-eds and anthology contributions. *Waiting for Scotland* is her second full-length poetry collection. She shares life with her husband, Tim, and their corgis, Edmund and Lillibette. Borders-Shoemaker is also an avid equestrian and can often be found riding her mustang, Rosa.

CPSIA information can be obtained
at www.ICGtesting.com
Printed in the USA
LVHW101624070123
736689LV00006B/701